ENDURING WORDS

FOR COUPLES

Daily Thoughts Suited
for Couples from
God's Enduring Word

By David Guzik
with Ruth Gordon

*The grass withers, the flower fades,
but the word of our God stands forever.*
Isaiah 40:8

Enduring Words for Couples
Copyright ©2021 by David Guzik
Complied and Edited by Ruth Gordon
ISBN 978-1-939466-62-4

Printed in the United States of America or in the United Kingdom

Enduring Word
5662 Calle Real #184
Goleta, CA 93117

Electronic Mail: ewm@enduringword.com
Internet Home Page: www.enduringword.com

All rights reserved. No portion of this book may be reproduced in any form (except for quotations in reviews) without the written permission of the publisher.
Scripture references, unless noted, are from the New King James Version of the Bible, copyright © 1979, 1980, 1982, Thomas Nelson, Inc., Publisher.

For Inga-Lill
my friend and my spouse

A FEW WORDS FROM THE AUTHOR

Life as a married couple should be life shared together – including our spiritual life.

My hope is that as couples spend daily time building their spiritual life, these short devotionals can be part of a stronger bond between husand and wife, and those who will become husband and wife.

David Guzik
January, 2021
Santa Barbara, California

ONE

What to Look for First

Therefore do not worry, saying, "What shall we eat?" or "What shall we drink?" or "What shall we wear?" For after all these things the Gentiles seek. For your heavenly Father knows that you need all these things. But seek first the kingdom of God and His righteousness, and all these things shall be added to you. Therefore do not worry about tomorrow, for tomorrow will worry about its own things. Sufficient for the day *is* its own trouble. (Matthew 6:31-34)

Therefore do not worry. Jesus invited us to know freedom from the anxiety caused by undue concern about material things. Most of our worry is over things that we have no control over anyway.

What shall we eat? or **What shall we drink?** or **What shall we wear?** We should live a higher life because **after all these things the Gentiles seek**. Jesus contrasted the life of those who do not know God and those who know God. Jesus didn't just tell us to stop worrying; He told us to *replace* worry with a concern for the kingdom of God. We can only abandon a passion or habit for a more significant passion or habit.

And all these things shall be added to you. If you put God's kingdom first, then you may enjoy **all these**

things: heavenly treasure, rest in divine provision, and fulfillment of God's highest purpose for man - fellowship with Him and being part of His kingdom.

Sufficient for the day is its own trouble. It isn't wrong to remember the past or plan for the future. Just don't ignore **the day** and **its own trouble**.

Prayer:

Lord, we need to return to **seek first the kingdom of God**. This must be the rule of our lives. It is the fundamental decision we made when we first repented and were converted. Please remind us to rightly prioritize our lives. Amen.

TWO

Illustrating the Principle with Humor

And why do you look at the speck in your brother's eye, but do not consider the plank in your own eye? Or how can you say to your brother, 'Let me remove the speck from your eye'; and look, a plank *is* in your own eye? Hypocrite! First remove the plank from your own eye, and then you will see clearly to remove the speck from your brother's eye. (Matthew 7:3-5)

Why do you look at the speck in your brother's eye, but do not consider the plank in your own eye? The figures of a **speck** and a **plank** are real figures yet used humorously. Jesus showed how we are generally far more tolerant of our sins than others' sins.

One example of looking for a speck in another's eye while ignoring the plank in one's own is when the religious leaders brought the woman taken in adultery to Jesus. She had undoubtedly sinned, but their sin was much worse than hers was, and Jesus exposed it as such with the statement, *He who is without sin among you, let him throw a stone at her first* (John 8:7).

Look, a plank is in your own eye. Jesus indicated that the one with the **plank in** his **own eye** would not immediately be aware of it. He is blind to his obvious fault. It is the attempt to correct the fault of someone else when we have the same (or greater fault) that earns the accusation, **Hypocrite!** That is a strong word but rightly said.

Our hypocrisy in these matters is almost always more evident to others than to ourselves. We may find a way to ignore the plank in our own eye, but others notice it immediately.

Prayer:

Father, Jesus didn't say that it was wrong for us to help each other with the speck in our brother's eyes, just *not before* dealing with the plank in our own eye. Please help us to not point out each other's faults without first examining our own. Amen.

THREE

The Word of the God Who Seeks Us

**Let my soul live, and it shall praise You;
And let Your judgments help me.
I have gone astray like a lost sheep;
Seek Your servant,
For I do not forget Your commandments.**
(Psalm 119:175-176)

"**Let my soul live, and it shall praise You; And let Your judgments help me.**" The psalmist recognized that his **soul** needed both *life* from God and *guidance* from God's word. With this combination of life and guidance, he would build a healthy relationship with God.

The ending section emphasizes the psalmist's great need for God and his dependence upon Him. His love for and dedication to the word of God has not made him more spiritually *independent* but more spiritually *dependent* upon God. He needed:

- Understanding (119:169)
- Deliverance (119:170)
- Ability to worship God rightly (119:171-172)
- Power to live an upright life (119:173-174)
- Strength to persevere (119:175)

I have gone astray like a lost sheep. The psalmist remembered his own frailty and sinful tendencies (**astray like a lost sheep**) and asked God to **seek** him.

He was like a **lost sheep** that will wander further and further from home until the shepherd finds and restores him.

Seek Your servant. He acknowledged that he was lost and needed God to **seek** him out – so he was poor, lost, and weak. He was also a **servant** of God and asked for help on that basis.

Prayer:

Lord, there is great power and glory in that You come to us and seek us through Your word. Let our souls live, and we will praise You. Amen.

FOUR

What God Is

God is love. (1 John 4:8)

Love describes the character and heart of God. He is so rich in love and compassion that this word can be used to describe His very being. When we say, **God is love**, we are not saying everything about God. Love is an essential aspect of His character and colors every aspect of His nature.

But God's love does not eliminate His holiness, His righteousness, or His perfect justice. Instead, we know the holiness of God is loving, and the righteousness of God is loving, and the justice of God is loving. Everything God does, in one way or another, expresses His love.

Because **God is love**, it means that there is always hope and forgiveness with Him.

While we shout, **God is love**, problems come when we try to say, "love is God." This is because love does not define everything in the character of God. It's also true because when most people use the term "love," they are not thinking of true love, the God-kind of love. Instead, they think of a soft, weak, "have-a-nice-day" kind of love that values being nice more than wanting what is truly best for the other person.

The Bible also tells us that God is "spirit" (John 4:24), that God is "light" (1 John 1:5), and that God is "a consuming fire" (Hebrews 12:29). Each of these things truly describes God, but no single term can describe Him completely.

Prayer:

Lord, help us to believe that **God is love**. We want to receive Your love and let it transform our lives. We ask You to help us stop trying to make ourselves worthy of Your love, and receive it, and then we will walk in the light and glory of Your love. Amen.

FIVE

Well Known, Yet Often Misunderstood

Judge not, that you be not judged. For with what judgment you judge, you will be judged; and with the measure you use, it will be measured back to you. (Matthew 7:1-2)

Judge not, that you be not judged. Most people seem to think that Jesus commanded a universal acceptance of any lifestyle or teaching. Jesus' words and context show that *is not* what He meant.

The Christian is called to show unconditional love but not called to unconditional *approval*. We *can* love people who do things that we disapprove of.

Judge not, that you be not judged. Jesus warned against passing judgment upon others because when we do so, we will be **judged** similarly. So while this does not prohibit examining others' lives, it indeed prohibits doing so with the wrong spirit.

For with what judgment you judge, you will be judged. Jesus only required that our judgment be entirely fair and judge others by a standard we would also like to be judged.

With the measure you use, it will be measured back to you: This is the principle upon which Jesus built the command, **Judge not, that you be not judged**. This is a powerful motivation for us to be generous with love, forgiveness, and goodness to others.

Some rabbis in Jesus' time taught that God had two measures that He used to judge people. One was a **measure** of *justice*, and the other was a **measure** of *mercy*. Whichever **measure** you want God to use with you, you should use that same **measure** with others.

Prayer:

Lord, we see that Jesus didn't prohibit all judgment. Yet, we should only judge another's behavior when we are mindful that *we will be judged* and consider how we would want to be judged. Amen.

SIX

Submit to God

But He gives more grace. Therefore He says: "God resists the proud, but gives grace to the humble." Therefore submit to God. Resist the devil and he will flee from you. (James 4:6-7)

First, **He gives more grace**. Next, **God resists the proud**. Then, God **gives grace to the humble**.

Knowing what God gives and who He resists, we are told what to do. **Therefore submit to God**. In light of the grace offered to the humble, there is only one thing to do: **submit to God**. This means to order yourself under God, to surrender to Him as a conquering King, and start receiving the benefits of His reign.

It is an amazing thing that the world does not submit to God. We often hear of the rights of man but what about the rights of God? He created beings who would not see if He had not given them eyes, and the creatures use those eyes to look everywhere except to God in heaven. He created beings that could not think apart from the minds He gave them, yet many of them think about everything except God.

God is a loving, giving Father; it is only dishonor and ingratitude to rebel against Him. Instead, Charles

Spurgeon suggested reasons why we should **submit to God**:

- We should submit to God because He created us.
- We should submit to God because His rule is good for us.
- We should submit to God because all resistance to Him is futile.
- We should submit to God because such submission is absolutely necessary to salvation.
- We should submit to God because it is the only way to have peace with God.

Prayer:

Lord, if we are not submitting to You, then we are submitting to Your adversary. If we don't submit to You, we will never be able to resist the devil. We both have a master; please help us to choose ours wisely. Amen.

SEVEN

Open Your Grief

And the prayer of faith will save the sick, and the Lord will raise him up. And if he has committed sins, he will be forgiven. Confess *your* trespasses to one another, and pray for one another, that you may be healed. The effective, fervent prayer of a righteous man avails much. (James 5:15-16)

Confess your trespasses to one another, and pray for one another, that you may be healed. Mutual confession and prayer bring physical and spiritual healing. Confession can free us from the heavy burdens of unresolved sin and removes hindrances to the work of the Holy Spirit.

To one another. Confession to each other in the body of Christ is important because sin isolates us from others. Confession breaks the power of secret sin. Confession of sin is good but must be made with discretion. An unwise confession of sin can be the cause of more sin.

Sin should especially be confessed where physical healing is necessary. It is possible - though not always the case - that a person's sickness is the result of some sin that has not been dealt with, as Paul describes in 1 Corinthians 11:30.

When sin is confessed, we must do it with *honesty and integrity*. If we confess with no intention of battling the sin, our confession isn't thorough, and it mocks God. *By all means, avoid phony confession - confession without true brokenness or sorrow. If it isn't authentic, it isn't any good.*

Those who hear a confession of sin also have a great responsibility and should have the proper response: loving intercessory prayer, not human wisdom, gossiping, or "sharing" the need with others.

Prayer:

Lord, we have learned that there can be a great value in *opening our grief* and **confessing *our* trespasses to one another**. We believe You will never despise it, and it often brings wonderful healing. Please help us to pray effectively and fervently for each other. Amen.

EIGHT

Why We Don't Get Along

Where do wars and fights *come* from among you? Do *they* not *come* from your *desires for* pleasure that war in your members? You lust and do not have. You murder and covet and cannot obtain. You fight and war. Yet you do not have because you do not ask. (James 4:1-2)

James accurately described strife with the terms **wars and fights**. He is referring to the battles that happen *among* Christians. Sadly, these battles are often bitter and severe.

Do they not come from your desires for pleasure that war in your members? The source of **wars and fights** among Christians is always the same. There is some root of carnality, an internal **war** within the believer regarding the lusts of the flesh.

Almost all who have a critical and contentious attitude claim the Spirit of God prompts them, but James makes it clear that this contention comes **from your desires**. *Covetousness* leads to conflict (**you lust and do not have**). *Anger* and *animosity* lead to hatred and conflict (**murder**). James referred to the Sermon on the Mount when he used **murder** to express more than killing but also an inward condition of the heart (Matthew 5:21-22).

Yet you do not have. This points to the *futility* of a life lived for the **desires for pleasure**. Not only is it a life of conflict, but also a fundamentally *unsatisfied* life. This dissatisfaction is not because of a lack of effort; we work hard to fulfill these desires - **yet you do not have**.

Prayer:

Father, it would be much wiser for us to accept a sense of dissatisfaction with that desire now and discover that it doesn't have to be our master, demanding satisfaction at any cost. Please grant us the wisdom to accept this lack of satisfaction now, instead of after much painful and harmful sin with all its consequences. Amen.

NINE

Stand Still

Moses said to the people, "Do not be afraid. Stand still, and see the salvation of the Lord." (Exodus 14:13)

It didn't look good for Israel. Blocking the front of the people of Israel was the Red Sea. Behind them was the fast-charging Egyptian army. Between the two was a multitude, quickly losing faith in God. At this point, Moses had no idea how God would come through in the situation. All he knew was that God would undoubtedly rescue His people. In a sense, Moses knew they were in such a dire situation that God had to save Israel.

When we see that our only help is God, we are more likely to trust Him. Sometimes it is the little things that defeat us because they are the things we *think* we can do in our strength. Often when it comes to the big things we know only God can do, we trust Him more.

Moses looked at the desperate situation and spoke for the Lord when he told Israel, **Stand still**. "Stand still" is often the Lord's word to the believer in crisis.

- *Despair* will try and cast you down and keep you from standing.
- *Fear* will say to retreat instead of standing still.
- *Impatience* will say to do something now instead of standing still.

- *Presumption* will say to jump into the Red Sea before it is parted.

Instead of any of these options, God tells us to **stand**, and to stand **still**.

Are things pressing around you? Are you caught in the middle of impossible circumstances? In Job 37:14, Elihu gave good counsel: *Stand still and consider the wondrous works of God*.

Prayer:

Lord, help us make sure we are standing where You wants us to stand, standing on Your word, and standing on Your promises. Then we will **stand still** there, confident in You, and consider Your wondrous works. Amen.

TEN

Spiritual Sounding Excuses

Thus speaks the LORD of hosts, saying: "This people says, 'The time has not come, the time that the LORD's house should be built.'" (Haggai 1:2)

The Prophet Haggai spoke this after the exiles had been back in Jerusalem for 18 years - but the rebuilding of the temple laid idle for the last 14 years.

The work started gloriously, but after two years they stopped, mired in discouragement. The temple's foundation was laid, and the altar was restored, but the temple wasn't rebuilt yet. Still, God's people felt it wasn't time to resume work. There were some good reasons why they might say this:

- The land was still desolate after 70 years of neglect.
- The work was hard.
- They didn't have a lot of money (Haggai 1:6) or manpower.
- They suffered crop failures and drought (Haggai 1:10-11).
- Hostile enemies resisted the work (Ezra 4:1-5).
- They remembered easier times in Babylon.

The time has not come, the time that the Lord's house should be built. The people made their excuses sound spiritual. They couldn't speak against the *idea* of building the temple, so they spoke against its *timing*. Because of the significant obstacles against the work, God's people began to rationalize and decided that it wasn't time to rebuild after all.

This people. God spoke to His people this way instead of "*My* people." He saw their low priorities and spiritual sounding excuses and they weren't living like His people.

Prayer:

Lord, it's a little too easy to do - spiritual words can roll off our tongue without having any spiritual substance behind them. In this light, we pray. Please search our hearts and see where we may be covering up a problem with spiritual sounding words. Amen.

ELEVEN

A Road That Is Longer and Tougher, But Better

Then it came to pass, when Pharaoh had let the people go, that God did not lead them by way of the land of the Philistines, although that was near; for God said, "Lest perhaps the people change their minds when they see war, and return to Egypt." So God led the people around by way of the wilderness of the Red Sea. (Exodus 13:17-18)

Pharaoh finally let go and let the people of Israel leave Egypt. As Israel left Egypt, God had a road for them to travel.

In that day, travel between Egypt and the empires of the north and west was common, and the roads led through the area we know today as Israel. There were well-maintained and traveled roads that could take the children of Israel right to the Promised Land. But God didn't want them to take an easy road.

The coastal road was known as the *Via Maris*, which is translated as "the way of the sea." It was the shortest and most common way, but it was where Egypt's military outposts were. God knew the people of Israel weren't ready to face those fortresses, so He led them a different way.

God will never allow us to face more than we can bear with His wisdom and strength. 1 Corinthians 10:13

says, *No temptation has overtaken you except such as is common to man; but God is faithful, who will not allow you to be tempted beyond what you are able, but with the temptation will also make the way of escape, that you may be able to bear it.* If God takes us on a difficult road, we can trust that it isn't too difficult as we rely on His strength.

Prayer:

Lord, we thank You for Your goodness today. Sometimes, the longer and more challenging road really is the better road. Thank You for all the disasters You have kept us from when we couldn't even see the danger. Help us to trust You and always rely on Your strength. Amen.

TWELVE

Yes and No

But above all, my brethren, do not swear, either by heaven or by earth or with any other oath. But let your "Yes," be "Yes," and *your* "No," "No," lest you fall into judgment. (James 5:12)

Do not swear. In the time James wrote this, many Jews made distinctions between "binding oaths" and "non-binding oaths." Oaths that did not include the name of God were considered non-binding, and making those oaths was like "crossing your fingers behind your back" when telling a lie.

Some have taken this verse to be more than an emphasis on truth-telling and honesty – they take this as a prohibition of all oaths. The Bible only forbids the swearing of deceptive, unwise, or flippant oaths:

- The Apostle Paul made oaths (Romans 1:9, 2 Corinthians 1:23, Galatians 1:20, and 2 Thessalonians 2:5).
- Jesus spoke under oath in a court (Matthew 26:63-64).
- On occasion, God Himself swears oaths (such as in Luke 1:73, Hebrews 3:11, and Hebrews 6:13).

James told us that instead of swearing an oath to establish that you are telling the truth, we should **let your "Yes" be "Yes."** Having to swear or make oaths betrays the weakness of our word. It demonstrates that there is not enough weight in our character to confirm what we say. How much better it is to let your **"Yes," be "Yes"** and **"No," "No."**

Why? **Lest you fall into judgment**. This lack of character will be exposed at the judgment seat of Christ. This motivates us all the more to prepare for that judgment by our speaking with integrity.

Prayer:

Lord, do people believe our word when we say it? Is our "Yes" received as "Yes" and our "No" received as "No"? Sometimes we may be truthful, yet not believed – Jesus is the prime example of this. Help us to say what we mean and to mean what we say. Amen.

THIRTEEN

Getting Our Attention

So when the LORD saw that he turned aside to look, God called to him from the midst of the bush and said, "Moses, Moses!" And he said, "Here I am." (Exodus 3:4)

By the time God got the attention of Moses, he had lived as an obscure shepherd in the desert for forty years. At this point, his life was so humble that he didn't own the flock of sheep he watched over - they belonged to his father-in-law.

One day, Moses brought the sheep to Horeb, called "the mountain of God." This mountain was later called Mount Sinai. There, Moses saw something extraordinary: a bush burning but not being burnt up.

It is not uncommon for plants like this to spontaneously ignite out in that desert. But two things were distinctive about that bush. First, the Angel of the LORD appeared from the midst of the bush. Second, though the bush burned, the bush was not consumed by the fire.

It was a thorn-bush because the original Hebrew word means "to stick or to prick." Thorns are a figure of the curse because Adam was cursed to bring forth thorns and thistles from the earth, according to Genesis 3:18. So we have a scene where the curse was being burned (a picture of judgment) yet it was not being consumed (a picture of God's mercy and grace).

But the miraculous sight alone didn't accomplish God's purpose. God didn't speak to Moses until He had Moses' attention. It says it was **when the Lord saw that he turned** God spoke to Moses. There can be amazing, miraculous things going on all around us. But God often won't speak to us until we turn to Him and listen.

Prayer:

Lord, we want You to speak to us. We give You our full attention by turning ourselves toward Your word, and listening. Accomplish Your purpose in us by Your mercy and grace. Amen.

FOURTEEN

Earthly Wisdom - False Wisdom

But if you have bitter envy and self-seeking in your hearts, do not boast and lie against the truth. This wisdom does not descend from above, but *is* earthly, sensual, demonic. For where envy and self-seeking *exist,* confusion and every evil thing *are* there. (James 3:14-16)

Here, James wrote mostly to teachers and leaders among God's people, but not only to them. He wrote about how important it was for them to use their words for good and not evil, to build up instead of tearing down. Then James focused on how important it is for believers to live in wisdom. James described the character of earthly wisdom, in contrast to the heavenly wisdom all God's people should have.

Earthly wisdom is marked by **bitter envy and self-seeking**. These are the opposite of *the meekness of wisdom*. It refers to someone who has a critical, contentious, fight-provoking manner. Earthly wisdom knows how to use people, manipulate them, and get what one wants out of them.

James tells us, **Do not boast and lie against the truth**. Anyone who shows **bitter envy and self-seeking** should not deceive anyone - especially themselves - about how wise they are. They offer wisdom that is

earthly, **sensual**, and **demonic**. Their wisdom is more characteristic of the world, the flesh, and the devil than of God. **This wisdom** that James referred to is not true wisdom.

Finally, James described the fruit of this earthly wisdom: **Confusion and every evil thing**. The wisdom of the world, the flesh, and the devil may be able to accomplish things, but it is always tainted with **confusion and every evil thing**.

Prayer:

Father, we need Your help to pursue heavenly wisdom, which flows from Your word and Your nature. Please help us to understand that this wisdom isn't the same as the wisdom of this world, and that You call all Your people to live lives of godly wisdom. Amen.

FIFTEEN

Affliction and Revival

Consider my affliction and deliver me,
For I do not forget Your law.
Plead my cause and redeem me;
Revive me according to Your word.
(Psalm 119:153-154)

The psalmist who wrote, **Consider my affliction and deliver me**, didn't live in constant comfort and peace. Yet he knew what to do in those seasons of affliction – to cry out to God. Here, he didn't ask for deliverance, but God's attention to his problem.

For I do not forget Your law. In the lives of some, affliction drives them away from God and His word. For the psalmist, such troubled times moved him closer to God and His word.

Plead my cause and redeem me. This is courtroom language. The psalmist knew that he needed God to **plead** his **cause** and to **redeem** him.

Revive me according to Your word. The psalmist wanted to be made alive and have that life brought to him according to God's word.

- The word of God is a *source* of personal and corporate revival if we will read the word of God and do what it tells us to do – in prayer, repentance, and the pursuit of God with a whole heart.

- Revival itself is **according to** God's **word**. A genuine revival will honor and promote God's word.
- There may be a false revival. Assess purported claims of revival, asking: "Is this **according to** God's **word**?"

Prayer:

Lord, consider our situation and plead our cause. Please revive us according to Your word. We will not forget Your law. Amen.

SIXTEEN

More Than Just Saying Words

If someone says, "I love God," and hates his brother, he is a liar; for he who does not love his brother whom he has seen, how can he love God whom he has not seen? And this commandment we have from Him: that he who loves God must love his brother also. (I John 4:20-21)

We can say we love God all day, but how is it seen in our life? It is easy for someone to proclaim their love for God because that is more of a private relationship with an invisible God.

John rightly insists that our claim of loving God is false if we do not love our brother with tangible love.

By this crucial measure, Jesus said the world could evaluate our status as disciples – by our love for one another: *By this all will know that you are My disciples, if you have love for one another* (John 13:35).

Though love springs forth from our abiding relationship with God and comes from our being born of Him, there is also an essential aspect of our will involved. We are commanded to love our brothers and sisters in the family of God.

It is a choice of our will to draw upon that resource and give it out to others. So here we are given a command to love, **that he who loves God must love his brother also**.

Therefore, the excuse, "I just can't love that person," is invalid. If we are born of Him and are abiding in Him, the resources for love are there.

Prayer:

Lord, we want to learn to love You, Whom we cannot see, by loving Your children, whom we can see. Show us how to love You more by loving each other more today. Help us to respond to Your command with our will and whole being. Amen.

SEVENTEEN

Another Great 3:16

By this we know love, because He laid down His life for us. And we also ought to lay down our lives for the brethren. (I John 3:16)

Sometimes at public events, someone will hold a sign reading, "John 3:16." The person with the sign wants people to look up John 3:16, "For God so loved the world that He gave His only begotten Son, that whoever believes in Him should not perish but have everlasting life." It is a great passage, but it isn't the only great 3:16 in the Bible.

1 John 3:16 not only tells us about God's love for us, it also tells us how we should love one another: **And we also ought to lay down our lives for the brethren**.

Jesus loved in this way; we should have the same kind of love. Since we are sent with the same mandate Jesus was sent with (John 20:21), we must demonstrate our love by laying down our lives for the brethren.

We may be willing to **lay down** our lives in a dramatic, heroic gesture. But will we **lay aside** our lives in a daily, simpler way? John reminds us that love often involves sacrifice. Merely wishing to be more loving won't do because it won't sacrifice where it is needed.

For most of us, God calls us to lay down our lives piece by piece, little by little in small, but important ways every day. John told us to do the same thing we read in Philippians 2:3-4: *Let nothing be done through selfish ambition or conceit, but in lowliness of mind let each esteem others better than himself. Let each of you look out not only for his own interests, but also for the interests of others.*

Prayer:

Lord, how can we better show Your love by laying aside our lives for each other today? Please help us learn how better to look out for the interests of each other, not just our own interests. Amen.

EIGHTEEN

The Most Reasonable Thing You Can Do

"Come now, and let us reason together," says the Lord. (Isaiah 1:18)

What people don't regret is getting right with God. Why? Because it's the reasonable thing to do. That's why God, through the prophet Isaiah, says, **Come now, let us reason together**. The Lord God invites His people to come reason with Him. God's direction for us is reasonable.

What madness it is to reject and resist a God of infinite wisdom, infinite love, infinite grace, and infinite power! True reason will drive any honest man to the most humble adoration and submission towards God.

The book of Revelation (Revelation 4:6-8) tells us that the angels surrounding God's throne are covered with eyes, which speaks of their incredible ability to perceive and know. These are perhaps the most intelligent, rational beings God ever created, and they spend every moment of their existence lost in total praise, total adoration, and unconditional surrender to God. That is where the highest reason will drive us! It is just plain reasonable to follow God.

Have you ever once heard of an old Christian, on their deathbed, gathering their children and friends around, and saying: "Now friends, watch out for that

Christianity! I've followed Jesus my whole life, and I'm so sorry I did! What a waste that was!" What nonsense! Quite the contrary, we find that most Christians on their deathbed are trusting and loving God more than ever. It's just plain reasonable!

Prayer:

Lord, when we consider how reasonable it is to get right with You, it is all the more reason for us to "come now." You want the separation between us to be gone now. We know You don't want us to continue in our destructive path another moment. Please help us spend some time getting right with and enjoying our relationship with You and then with each other. Amen.

NINETEEN

Principles of Judgment

Now the king of Assyria went throughout all the land, and went up to Samaria and besieged it for three years. In the ninth year of Hoshea, the king of Assyria took Samaria and carried Israel away to Assyria. (2 Kings 17:5-6)

It took a three-year siege, but eventually, the **king of Assyria** conquered Israel, the kingdom of the ten northern tribes. This was a long campaign to finally crush Israel's rebellious kingdom, which had defied the power of the Assyrian Empire.

The walls surrounding Samaria were good enough to keep the enemy out for three years. But the strength of the walls couldn't stand against the judgment of God, and the Assyrian army was an instrument of God's judgment against Israel. When God brings His judgment, He *may use human instruments* to do it.

The Northern Kingdom of Israel didn't fall because God could not help them, but because they had so forsaken Him and ignored His guidance and correction, the Lord finally stopped protecting them according to their desire.

As they **carried Israel away to Assyria**, they led the captives away on journeys of hundreds of miles, naked and attached with strings and fishhooks through their lower lips. This shows another principle of God's judgment: It *may be humiliating and degrading* when it comes.

This should give us a sober fear of the judgment of God. Israel had enjoyed a heritage of rich blessing in the past, but that would not protect them from God's judgment if they continued to mock God and rebel against Him.

Prayer:

Lord, help us to not be rebellious against You. Grant us a deeper appreciation for Christ's death on the cross as our substitute for the judgment we deserve, that those trusting in Him would never face God's judgment. Amen.

TWENTY

Real but Unseen

So he answered, "Do not fear, for those who are with us are more than those who are with them." And Elisha prayed, and said, "LORD, I pray, open his eyes that he may see." Then the LORD opened the eyes of the young man, and he saw. And behold, the mountain was full of horses and chariots of fire all around Elisha. (2 Kings 6:16-17)

The king of Syria was at war against Israel and angry with Elisha, Israel's prophet. God spoke to Elisha about the plans of the Syrian army, and for a time, Israel knew every move the Syrians made. Furious, the king of Syria sent soldiers with many horses and chariots. They surrounded Elisha's city and demanded his surrender.

Elisha had perfect peace, but his servant was afraid, knowing there was little chance of escaping or surviving an attack from so many. Elisha told him not to be afraid – **those who are with us are more than those who are with them**. Elisha saw what his servant couldn't, and he prayed for the servant's eyes to be opened.

Elisha didn't pray that God would change the situation, only that his servant could see the reality. The servant couldn't have this explained to him, nor could he be persuaded into it. When a person is blind to spiritual reality, only God can open his eyes. God may use others' words, but the work of spiritually opening eyes is God's alone.

When God opened his eyes, the servant saw more with him and Elisha than those against them. God's protection of **chariots of fire** was real, though invisible.

Prayer:

Lord, please open our eyes to the spiritual reality around us and perceive what is real though unseen. We acknowledge this is our Father's world. Amen.

TWENTY-ONE

If Water Is Wet and Rocks Are Hard

Therefore if there is any consolation in Christ, if any comfort of love, if any fellowship of the Spirit, if any affection and mercy. (Philippians 2:1)

Paul's purpose is to help the Philippian church brethren get along better. He introduces the basis for unity, humility, and love among believers. If they have received the things in Philippians 2:1, then they have a responsibility to do what he is about to describe.

If there is any consolation in Christ. Is there any consolation in Christ? Of course, there is! Every Christian should know what it is to have Jesus console their soul. Luke 2:25 says Jesus is *the Consolation of Israel*. 2 Corinthians 1:5 says, *For as the sufferings of Christ abound in us, so our consolation also abounds through Christ*. 2 Thessalonians 2:16 says that God *has loved us and given us everlasting consolation and good hope by grace*.

If there is any...comfort of love. Is there any comfort of love? Of course, there is! 2 Corinthians 1:3 says God is the *God of all comfort*. There is no circumstance beyond His comfort. The word comfort here is the ancient Greek word *paraklesis*. The idea behind this word in the New Testament is strengthening, helping, and making strong. This word is communicated by the

Latin word for comfort (*fortis*), which means, "brave." The love of God in our life makes us strong and brave.

If there is any...fellowship of the Spirit. Is there any fellowship of the Spirit? Of course, there is! Every Christian should know what it is to have the fellowship of the Spirit. Fellowship is the ancient Greek word "koinonia." It means the sharing of things in common.

Prayer:

Lord, we know these things should be just as real in our life as the wetness of water, the hotness of fire, and the hardness of rocks. Please help us get along better by heeding these principles so we may share life with the Spirit of God that we never knew before. Amen.

TWENTY-TWO

Life Without Meaning

In the beginning, God created the heavens and the earth. (Genesis 1:1)

When we realize who God is and who we are, it sets a foundation for a life full of meaning.

Genesis 1:1 declares that the world did not create itself or come about by chance; **God created** it. He is eternal and has always been. If He created this world, and us He has a plan for both the world and us as individuals. We can find meaning in our lives by fulfilling the purpose our Creator has for us. When we look to His word, we discover what that purpose is.

Many people think Genesis 1:1 doesn't have anything to do with scientific fact. They look to other things for meaning in life. God is there, and it is only through Him that we discover the real purpose for our lives.

Some 100 years ago, there was a great German philosopher named Arthur Schopenhauer. By habit, he usually dressed like a bum, and one day he was sitting on a park bench in Berlin, deep in thought. His appearance made a policeman suspicious, so the policeman asked the philosopher, "Who are you?" Schopenhauer answered, "I would to God I knew."

And the only way we can ever really find out who we are is from God - and the place to begin is Genesis 1:1. Today, spend some special time considering what it means that God is your Creator, and you are His creatures.

Prayer:

Lord, we purpose to look to Your word to learn more about Your purpose for our lives. We know we have an important place in Your plan, and Jesus' death for us on the cross shows how important we are to You. Amen.

TWENTY-THREE

A Burden or Not?

For this is the love of God, that we keep His commandments. And His commandments are not burdensome. (1 John 5:3)

Most people think the commandments of God are a burden. How can John say, **His commandments are not burdensome**?

His commandments are not burdensome when we see how wise and good the commandments of God are. They are gifts from Him to show us the best and most fulfilling life possible. God's commands are like the "manufacture's handbook" for life. He tells us what to do because He knows how we work best. God's commands are not given to bind us, pain us, or because God is angry.

His commandments are not burdensome because when we are born again, we are given new hearts – hearts that by instinct wish to please God. The New Covenant states the law of God has been written on the heart of every believer (Jeremiah 31:33).

His commandments are not burdensome when we compare them to the religious rules men make up. John is not trying to say obedience is an easy thing. If that were so, it would be easy for us not to sin, and

John has already acknowledged that we all do sin (1 John 1:8).

Jesus said of Himself, *My yoke is easy and My burden is light* (Matthew 11:30). Instead of the burdensome requirement to keep hundreds of little rules and regulations, Jesus says to us, "Love Me and love My people, and you will walk in obedience."

Prayer:

Lord, obeying Your commands does not seem like a burden to us when we love You. When we love each other, it seems little trouble to go to a lot of difficulty to help or please each other. Please help us to enjoy obeying Your commands and loving each other without complaining. Amen.

TWENTY-FOUR

How to Make Big Decisions

Then they returned to Jerusalem from the mount called Olivet, which is near Jerusalem, a Sabbath day's journey. And when they had entered, they went up into the upper room where they were staying.... These all continued with one accord in prayer and supplication, with the women and Mary the mother of Jesus, and with His brothers. (Acts 1:12-14)

In Acts chapter 1, the disciples had a big decision to make - who would replace Judas as the twelfth apostle? Their steps in Acts 1:12-14 give us an example to follow before we make decisions.

Their *obedience* is notable; Jesus had told them to return to Jerusalem and wait for the coming of the Holy Spirit, and that is what they did even though He was no longer physically present with them. Making the right decisions begins with being obedient right now with what we know to be God's will.

Their *unity* is notable; **These all continued with one accord**. In the gospels, it seemed the disciples were always fighting. What had changed? Peter still had the history of denying the Lord; Matthew was still a tax collector; Simon was still a zealot. But the resurrected Jesus in their hearts was more significant than any of their differences. When we seek God in a big decision, disunity can get in the way. Being out of fellowship, either through our absence or bad relationship - puts us in the wrong place for decision-making.

Their *prayer* is notable; they all prayed, and they **continued in prayer and supplication**; the idea of supplication is a sense of desperation and earnestness in prayer. They were depending on God and showing that dependence in a radical way - through earnest prayer.

Prayer:

Lord, help us make good, godly decisions; but we know these are essential for a good foundation: obedience, unity, and prayer. We know now is the time to grow stronger in these three areas before the time for a big decision comes. Amen.

TWENTY-FIVE

Happy People or New Men?

You will show me the path of life; in Your presence is fullness of joy; at Your right hand are pleasures forevermore. (Psalm 16:11)

There was a time in our world when the most important question was, "How can I be right with God." Now, for most people, the most important question is, "How can I be happy?"

The idolatry of a happy life is as present among Christians as anywhere else. We judge the goodness of things around us based on how happy it all makes us. God's greatest purpose in our lives is not to make us happy but to transform us into godly people - people who are like Jesus. *For whom He foreknew, He also predestinated to be conformed to the image of His Son* (Romans 8:29)

God loves us too much to allow us to worship at the altar of the "happy life" for very long. He has a way of bringing circumstances about which force us to focus more on godliness than happiness. If that's where your life is right now, don't resent it. Don't think that God wants you to be unhappy. That isn't it. It's just that He cares more about your godliness than your happiness.

This is the great secret of life: happiness is most securely achieved when we put godliness first. Happiness is like a bluebird that flies about, and if we set our focus on chasing it, it just flies further away. But when we set our hearts on God and His kingdom, the bluebird of happiness will set right down on our shoulders.

Surely goodness and mercy shall follow me all the days of my life (Psalm 23:6). The psalmist wasn't concerned with chasing goodness and mercy but sought God and goodness and mercy followed.

Prayer:

Lord, we know when we seek You and Your kingdom first, You will take care of our happiness. Please help us spend more time in Your presence and find our joy there, not from the world and its fleeting illusions. Amen.

TWENTY-SIX

Another Reason to Be Fair to Everyone

If you really fulfill *the* royal law according to the Scripture, "You shall love your neighbor as yourself," you do well; but if you show partiality, you commit sin, and are convicted by the law as transgressors. (James 2:8-9)

James understood the danger of partiality among the people of God. When race, class, wealth, social standing, education, or more divides them, it's a terrible thing. Those divisions are bad in society, but they are even worse among those who claim to belong to Jesus. He meant for His followers to be one and not to be divided by superficial lines.

James writes, **If you really fulfill the royal law according to the Scripture**. James anticipated some of his readers might defend their partiality to the rich as loving them as their neighbor in obedience to the law.

If you show partiality, you commit sin. The problem isn't that one is too nice to the rich. The problem is that one does **show partiality** to the rich and is not nice to the poor man! So you can't excuse your **partiality** by saying, "I'm just fulfilling the command to love my neighbor as myself."

When we love everyone – not showing partiality – we are fulfilling God's **royal law**. Our God is a great King, and His law is a **royal law**. Our King Jesus emphasized this command (Matthew 22:36-40) from the Old Testament (Leviticus 19:18). James is reminding us that the poor man is just as much as our **neighbor** as the rich man is.

Prayer:

Lord, if we would fulfill this **royal law**, we know it doesn't mean loving someone less but loving others more. As we see in the Old Testament and the words of Jesus, we love everyone as our neighbor – especially those in the family of God and each other. We want You to be able to say of us, "**You do well**." Amen.

TWENTY-SEVEN

One or the Other?

In this the children of God and the children of the devil are manifest: Whoever does not practice righteousness is not of God, nor is he who does not love his brother. (I John 3:10)

A frightened woman was dragged before Jesus. Her accusers had an airtight case: she was caught in the act of adultery. The righteousness of the law said, "Execute her by stoning." Jesus looked at the woman with holy love and saw she was a pawn in the hands of men trying to attack Him. The love of God said, "Let her go."

Which would it be, righteousness or love? Righteousness without love makes one a religious Pharisee, and love without righteousness makes one a partner in evil.

So, how do the two balance out? They don't. They aren't opposites. We are never to love at the expense of righteousness, nor be righteous at the expense of love. Real love is the greatest righteousness, and real righteousness is the greatest love.

When Jesus was confronted with a choice between righteousness and love, He acted according to His nature – the nature of God: perfect love, perfect righteousness. He did not say the woman was guiltless. Nor did Jesus throw the first stone for her execution. Jesus focused on the greater evil of the men who brought the woman. He asked if there were a guiltless one among them to cast the first stone, and they all declined, dropped the matter, and left.

Did this mean her sin was unimportant? No! Jesus told her: "go and sin no more."

Prayer:

Lord, when people look at our lives, do they see both love and righteousness? We know either one alone is not enough. If they can see both, they see the nature of Jesus in us. Please help us to demonstrate His love and His righteousness in our lives today. Amen.

TWENTY-EIGHT

Just Do It

Therefore, to him who knows to do good and does not do *it*, to him it is sin. (James 4:17)

James challenges us to live according to what we know in the Lord.

To him who knows to do good and does not do it, to him it is sin. James knew that it is far easier to *think about* and *talk about* humility and dependence on God than to live them. Yet he made the mind of God plain: we are accountable to *do them*, as we know these things.

James says that genuine faith is proved by action. You might have a great opinion of God's word and be skilled in memorizing or interpreting it. Yet at the end of it all, the question is: Do you *do* it? If you know **to do good** and do **not do it**, then **it is sin**.

In the previous passage, James reminded us of life's uncertainty and how we should not make our plans without a humble dependence upon God.

Here, James wants to remind us that this humility should not create fear that makes us passive or inactive. The uncertainty of life should make us ready to recognize what is **good** and then **do it**.

If we see the good to do and then do not do it, then **to him it is sin**. Jesus said: *For everyone to whom much is given, from him much will be required; and to whom much has been committed, of him they will ask the more.* (Luke 12:48)

Prayer:

Lord, because we have been given greater light, we have a greater responsibility. We know a lot of good to do – now please give us the strength to do it. Amen.

TWENTY-NINE

Don't Give Up

Now therefore, I urge you, give a pledge to my master the king of Assyria, and I will give you two thousand horses—if you are able on your part to put riders on them! (2 Kings 18:23)

The armies of Assyria crushed the northern neighbor of Judah, and then cruelly carried away the ten northern tribes of Israel. Now those soldiers surrounded the city of Jerusalem after having conquered virtually everything else in Judah.

The general commanding the armies of Assyria – who had the title "The Rabshakeh" – gave a long, public speech in the hearing of Hezekiah, the king of Judah. The Assyrian general told Hezekiah that Judah was already defeated, Jerusalem surrounded, and there was no hope or point resisting any longer.

Judah had trusted in a partnership with Egypt – the Rabshakeh told Hezekiah it would fail. Some in Judah thought Yahweh, the covenant God of Israel, would rescue them – but the Rabshakeh told them there was no use in trusting God. He even said that God was mad at them and would never defend them! The Rabshakeh offered to give Hezekiah **two thousand horses** – but even that wouldn't help them. He also said that he was actually on a mission from God to conquer Judah. The Rabshakeh's strategy was to *make Hezekiah give up*.

The enemy of our soul uses the same approach. Satan doesn't want to battle with you but instead *talk you into giving up because:*

- There is a strong chance you will win.
- Win or lose, the battle can draw you closer to Jesus.
- What Jesus does through the struggle, can bless others.

Prayer:

Lord, help us stand together against Satan and his lies in the name of Jesus! Give us Your strength, never to give in or give up! Amen.

THIRTY

Wasting Strength

Finally, my brethren, be strong in the Lord and in the power of His might. (Ephesians 6:10)

It's a powerful statement from the Apostle Paul – an invitation for us to draw on the resources of God's strength. That's more than enough strength for any of us.

Yet, there is an aspect to this that we must consider. I first found the connection to this verse from the works of the late Dr. Martyn Lloyd-Jones.

In his excellent sermon series on this text, Dr. Lloyd-Jones listed many ways he believed Christians wasted their strength. It was as if they had received some of the available might of God, but it merely leaked away like water in a bucket full of holes.

- Committing to too many spiritual works or things
- Too much conversation
- Arguments, debates, wrangling
- Laziness
- Too much time in the wrong company
- Too much foolish talk and joking
- Love of money and career
- A desire for respectability and image
- An unequal partnership with an unbeliever

- Ungodly entertainment
- A wrong attitude toward or doubting the Word of God

Ask God what might apply to your life. Lloyd-Jones wrote: "We have to walk on a knife-edge in these matters; you must not become extreme on one side or the other. But you have to be watchful."

Prayer:

Lord, we purpose to examine ourselves whether our strength is increasing or declining. We know we must receive our strength from You. Please help us not to waste it. Amen.

THIRTY-ONE

Now Stop That Fighting!

Whoever believes that Jesus is the Christ is born of God, and everyone who loves Him who begot also loves him who is begotten of Him. (1 John 5:1)

John often mentions being **born of God** (as in 1 John 2:29, 3:9, and 4:7). Here he told us how one is born of God: **Whoever believes that Jesus is the Christ**. We believe Jesus is the Christ when we trust that He is our Messiah, not just the Messiah in the generic sense, but by trust and faith in Him. John's great emphasis has been on love, but he never wants anyone to believe they earn salvation by loving others.

We also understand that John did not mean a mere intellectual agreement that Jesus is the Messiah. Even demons might do this much (James 2:19). But we need to have a trust in and reliance on Jesus as Messiah. Additionally, John makes it clear we must believe **Jesus is the Christ**.

Being born of God also affects our lives: it is assumed that we will love God (**Him who begot us**) because we are born again into His family. But it is also assumed that we will love others begotten of Him - our brothers and sisters in the family of Jesus. This new birth is the common ground of Christians. Not race, not class, not culture, not a language, or any other thing except a common birth in Jesus Christ, and the common Lordship of Jesus.

To love all others in the family of God means that you do not limit your love to your denomination or group, to your own social or financial status, to your race, to your political perspective, or your exact theological persuasion.

Prayer:

Lord, forgive us if any of these things mean more to us than our common salvation and the common Lordship of Jesus Christ. Please help us to better love each other and all in the family of God. Amen.

Scripture Index

Genesis 1:1	Day 22
Exodus 3:4	Day 13
Exodus 13:17-18	Day 11
Exodus 14:13	Day 9
2 Kings 6:16-17	Day 20
2 Kings 17:5-6	Day 19
2 Kings 18:23	Day 29
Psalm 16:11	Day 25
Psalm 119:153-154	Day 15
Psalm 119:175-176	Day 3
Isaiah 1:18	Day 18
Haggai 1:2	Day 10
Matthew 6:31-34	Day 1
Matthew 7:3-5	Day 2
Matthew 7:1-2	Day 5
Acts 1:12-14	Day 24
Ephesians 6:10	Day 30
Philippians 2:1	Day 21
James 2:8-9	Day 26
James 3:14-16	Day 14
James 4:1-2	Day 8
James 4:6-7	Day 6
James 4:17	Day 28
James 5:12	Day 12
James 5:15-16	Day 7
I John 3:10	Day 27
I John 3:16	Day 17
I John 4:8	Day 4
I John 4:20-21	Day 16
1 John 5:1	Day 31
1 John 5:3	Day 23

Title List

A Burden or Not?	Day 23
A Road That Is Longer, Tougher, But Better	Day 11
Affliction and Revival	Day 15
Another Great 3:16	Day 17
Another Reason to Be Fair to Everyone	Day 26
Earthly Wisdom - False Wisdom	Day 14
Don't Give Up	Day 29
Getting Our Attention	Day 13
Happy People or New Men?	Day 25
How To Make Big Decisions	Day 24
If Water Is Wet and Rocks Are Hard	Day 21
Illustrating the Principle with Humor	Day 2
Just Do It	Day 28
Life Without Meaning	Day 22
More Than Just Saying Words	Day 16
The Most Reasonable Thing You Can Do	Day 18
Now Stop That Fighting!	Day 31
One or the Other?	Day 27
Open Your Grief	Day 7
Principles of Judgment	Day 19
Real but Unseen	Day 20
Spiritual Sounding Excuses	Day 10
Stand Still	Day 9
Submit to God	Day 6
Wasting Strength	Day 30
Well Known Yet Often Misunderstood	Day 5
What to Look for First	Day 1
What God Is	Day 4
Why We Don't Get Along	Day 8
The Word of the God Who Seeks Us	Day 3
Yes and No	Day 12

Topical Index

Affliction
Day 15

Angels
Day 18

Anger
Day 8

Blessing
Day 19

Comfort, Encouragement
Days 21, 15

Confession
Day 7

Covenant
Days 23, 29

Creator
Day 22

The Cross
Days 19, 21, 22

Danger, Warning
Days 5, 11, 26

Direction
Day 18

Discouragement
Day 10

Faith
Days 9, 28, 31

Faithfulness
Day 11

Fear
Days 9, 19, 20, 28

Forgiveness
Days 4, 5, 7, 31

Freedom
Days 1, 7

Glory
Days 3, 4

God
Days 4, 5, 6, 8, 9, 10, 11, 12, 13, 14, 15, 16, 17, 18, 19, 20, 21, 22, 23, 24, 25, 26, 27, 28, 29, 30, 31

God's Word
Days 3, 15, 28

Gospel
Day 24

Grace
Days 6, 13, 18, 21

The Heart
Days 4, 8, 10, 14, 15, 23, 24, 25

Heaven, Heavenly
Days 1, 6, 12, 14, 22

Holiness
Day 4

Holy Spirit
Days 7, 24

Hope
Days 4. 21, 29

Humility, Humble
Days 6, 13, 18, 21, 28

Hypocrisy
Day 2

Idolatry
Day 25

Israel
Days 9, 19, 20, 29

Israel in the Exodus
Days 9, 11

Jesus' Nature
Days 1, 2, 3, 12, 16, 17, 21, 23, 24, 25, 26, 27, 28, 29, 31

Joy
Day 25

Judgment
Days 3, 5, 12, 13, 19

Light
Days 4, 26, 28

Love
Days 3, 4, 5, 16, 18, 21, 23, 25, 26, 27, 31

Meekness
Day 14

Mercy
Days 5, 13, 21, 25

Obedience
Days 23, 24, 26

Patience
Day 9

Peace
Days 6, 15, 20

Power of Words
Days 5, 10, 14, 16, 20

Praise, Worship
Days 3, 18, 25

Prayer
Days 7, 15, 24

Pride, Proud
Day 6

Priorities
Days 1, 10

Promises
Day 9

Protection
Days 19, 20

Religion, Religious
Days 2, 27, 23

Repentance
Days 1, 15

Restoration, Revival
Days 3, 15

Resurrection
Day 24

Righteousness
Days 1, 4, 7, 27

Salvation
Days 6, 9, 31

Satan
Day 29

Sermon on the Mount
Day 8

Sin
Days 2, 3, 7, 8, 23, 26, 27, 28

Spiritual Warfare
Days 8, 29

Strength
Days 9, 11, 21, 28, 29, 30

Truth
Days 12, 14

Wealth, Riches
Days 1, 30

Wisdom
Days 7, 8, 14, 18

Worldliness
Days 6, 14, 16, 25

Thank you to my wife Inga-Lill, with whom this year I celebrate 38 years of marriage. I'm grateful that we have been strengthened year by year through prayer and God's word.

Thanks also to Brian Procedo for his graphic design, and especially to Ruth Gordon, who has edited and compiled these devotionals.

David Guzik's Bible commentary is regularly used and trusted by many thousands who want to know the Bible better. Pastors, teachers, class leaders, and everyday Christians find his commentary helpful for their own understanding and explanation of the Bible. David and his wife Inga-Lill live in Santa Barbara, California and have three adult children and two grandchildren.

You can email David at **david@enduringword.com**

For more resources by David Guzik, go to
www.enduringword.com

www.ingramcontent.com/pod-product-compliance
Lightning Source LLC
Chambersburg PA
CBHW031417040426
42444CB00005B/616